CIM REVISION CARDS
Delivering Customer Value

Ray Donnelly

ELSEVIER

AMSTERDAM • BOSTON • HEIDELBERG • LONDON • NEW YORK • OXFORD
PARIS • SAN DIEGO • SAN FRANCISCO • SINGAPORE • SYDNEY • TOKYO

Butterworth-Heinemann is an imprint of Elsevier
Linacre House, Jordan Hill, Oxford OX2 8DP
30 Corporate Drive, Burlington, MA 01803

British Library Cataloguing in Publication Data
A Catalogue record for this book is available from the British Library

Library of Congress Cataloging in Publication Data
A Catalog record for this book is available from the Library of Congress

ISBN: 978-1-85617-851-8

For information on all Butterworth-Heinemann publications visit our website at www.elsevierdirect.com

Printed and bound in Great Britain
09 10 11   11 10 9 8 7 6 5 4 3 2 1

Working together to grow
libraries in developing countries

www.elsevier.com | www.bookaid.org | www.sabre.org

ELSEVIER   BOOK AID International   Sabre Foundation

TABLE OF CONTENTS

NEW PRODUCT DEVELOPMENT AND POSITIONING

Chapter 1

LEARNING OUTCOMES

Examine the value and contribution of effective product management

➡ Apply the new product development process
➡ Assess product positioning and how it is applied

KEY REVISION POINTS

➡ What is a product and the types of new product?
➡ Understanding the NPD process
➡ Product adoption categories
➡ The role of innovation

Syllabus reference: 1.1, 1.3 and 1.4

REVISION TIPS

Your exam will require you to demonstrate four elements:

- Concept (40%)
- Application (30%)
- Evaluation (20%)
- Presentation (10%)

The CIM refers to the above as the 'magic formula' and your exam will be marked against these overall criteria.

You should plan your revision so that you can reflect on the entire syllabus (not just parts of it). Do not leave to the last moment, rather revise each section of the syllabus as you complete it.

Write down a revision timetable and stick to it. Make it realistic, so that it fits in with the other things you need to do and keep a sense of balance.

Understand the theories by relating them to an organisation and study beyond the text books. Consider *The Economist*, quality newspapers or their websites and Radio 4 (business programmes) to give you a broad perspective. The CIM website is also very helpful.

What Is a Product?

The terms product and services are used interchangeably, but they do have precise definitions and implications which helps marketers be more effective in carrying out their roles.

Kotler (1999) defines a product as 'anything that is offered to the market for attention, acquisition, use or consumption that might satisfy a need or want'. He defines a service as 'products that consist of activities, benefits, or satisfactions that are offered for sale that are essentially intangible and do not result in the ownership of anything'.

A product can be a physical good, service, idea or indeed a person. In other words, a product is something that is capable of meeting customers' needs.

There are three product levels:

Summary of product levels	
The core product	This is the basic product, i.e. what the customer is buying. Marketers define the core product elements in meaningful customer terms.
The actual product	Is composed of several characteristics such as styling, brand, quality, and packaging.
The augmented product	Additional consumer benefits/services are added, including (for example) warranties, guarantees, and dedicated help lines.

Product Categories

Products can be categorised into consumer and business products with the key differentiator being the purpose for which the product is to be used.

The New Product Development (NPD) Process

There are seven stages (testing and launch are often be separate) in the process which are illustrated in the following diagram.

Each stage of the process needs to be carefully managed to ensure that only the most relevant products with the highest chance of success are perused. Most new products actually fail and the development costs wasted.

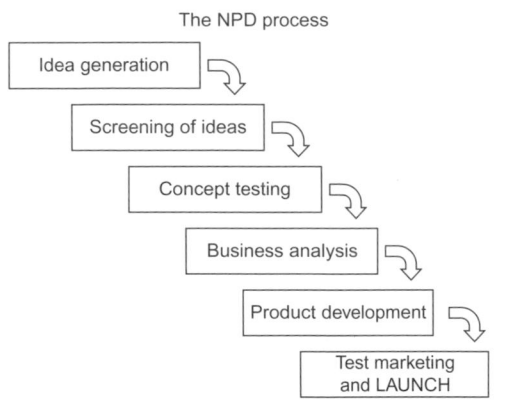

The NPD process

Types of New Product

There are different types of newness for a product, and Brassington and Pettitt (2006) suggests four types:

- New to company and market
  - This is a totally new product which has never been offered before. At one time, mobile phones would have come under this category
- New to company, significant innovation for market
  - Core product is familiar to the consumer, but an additional feature has been added
- New to company, minor innovation for market
  - Burden is now on the company and the launch of the product is unlikely to have a significant impact on the market
- New to company, no innovation for market
  - 'me too' products often when a market follower launches a product into the market

Product Standardisation or Adaptation

Organisations that operate outside their domestic market must consider the implications for standardising or adapting their products.

Where the product is standardised, an organisation will offer the same product in each of the markets it serves, whereas with adaptation the product will be changed according to the needs of each market.

The different types of organisations involved in overseas activities are:

Organisation	Summary
International	Domestic marketing mix applied to all countries in which it operates.
Multinational	Each overseas market is regarded as a discrete area which reports into the home country head office.
Global	Organisations that have a single marketing mix. A global rather than country approach is taken.

Product Positioning

A product's position is considered to be the way the product is defined by consumers on important attributes – the place the product occupies in consumers' mind relative to competing products.

Product Adoption

Product adoption refers to the various stages a consumer goes through as part of the process of purchasing a new product.

The adoption stages are:

Product adoption stages	Summary
1. Awareness	At this stage the consumer becomes aware of the product, but lacks information on it.
2. Interest	The consumer now seeks information on the product and this could be around features and benefits.
3. Evaluation	Is the product worth trying? Does it meet the needs of the consumer?
4. Trial	The consumer will now try the product; this could be by free sample, special promotion or free trial.
5. Adoption	The consumer tries to make full use of the product, although this does not offer any guarantee of loyalty.

Product Adoption Categories

Consumers do not take up a new product at the same rate and can be grouped into categories reflecting the rate at which the product is adopted.

Innovation

The process and technical aspects of developing new products, managing their position in changing markets and the relationship with the dynamic needs of customers have been considered. However, innovation brings these processes to life and enables excellent

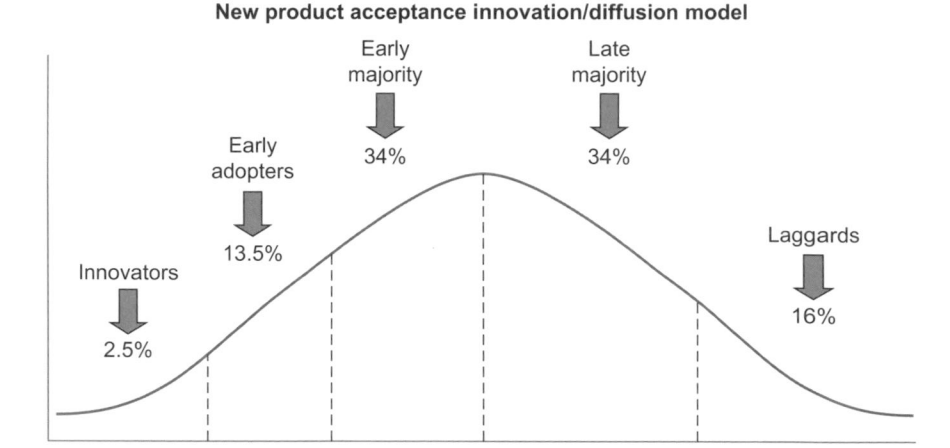

New product acceptance innovation/diffusion model

customer led NPD and management. Innovation comes from a variety of sources:

- Customers
- Front line staff
- Executives
- Advisers

Innovation is not just about bringing new products to the market. It is about reinventing business processes and building entirely new markets that meet untapped customer needs. Most important, as the Internet and globalisation widen the pool of new ideas, it is about selecting and executing the right ideas and bringing them to market in record time. (Business Week April 2006).

PRODUCT MANAGEMENT PROCESS

Chapter 2

LEARNING OUTCOMES

➡ Evaluate the main marketing tools used to manage individual products and product portfolios
➡ Apply product management tools and techniques in various organisational contexts

Syllabus reference: 1.1

KEY REVISION POINTS

➡ The role of portfolio management
➡ Understanding the PLC and BCG matrix

Portfolio Management

Few organisations have just one product to offer their customers and a range of products allows for segmentation, targeting and positioning (STP) of the portfolio, leading to a greater market share, higher levels of customer satisfaction and increased resilience for the organisation.

Additional products must be added in a systematic and logical way.

Product management is integral in creating value for customers, it does this through the effective management of the marketing mix (4/7Ps) in order to satisfy customer needs.

Marketing mix	Commentary
Product	The right product(s) available to meet current customer needs (added value). The product range can be expanded or collapsed as needs change.
Price	It is important to understand how customers perceive price, so the organisation must be clear on exactly how to price its products and the relationship with any other products within its portfolio.
Promotion	A range of tools is available to support the product, create customer satisfaction and loyalty through careful positioning in the customers mind. Branding reinforces the product image with the consumer.
Place	It is necessary to get the products to customers where they want to purchase, not where you would like them to purchase.
Physical evidence	Where services are concerned, some tangibility needs to be provided to support the overall proposition. This could range from brochures to the decor of the office where the service is delivered.
People	Arguably the most important element, who need to be consistent, professional and reflect the brand.
Processes	Important to train staff and have defined processes in place to support staff in delivering a consistent and a high quality service.

New products cannot simply be added to the organisations product portfolio in a random way; the table below sets out how organisations portfolio can be categorised.

Product mix	This is the total of all products (and variants) that an organisation offers to its customers.
Product line	Here, the product mix is divided and grouped into products which are related to each other for internal (production or technical reasons) or external reasons as they all offer a similar solution to the consumer.
Product item	The product line is further divided into individual products which meet a specific customer need.

The product life cycle (PLC) below shows sales and revenue plotted against time.

Product Life Cycle

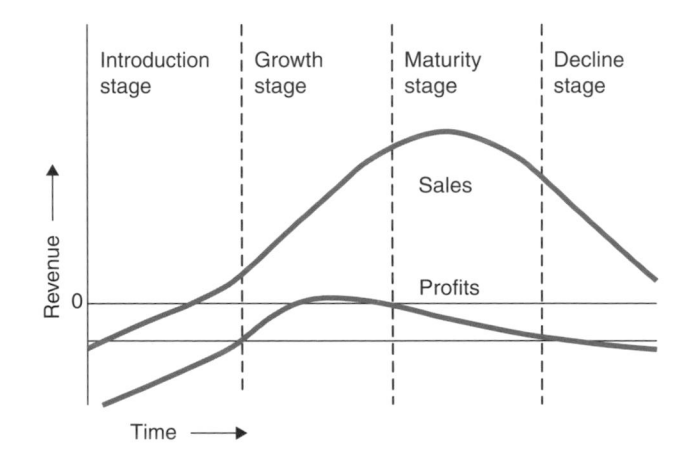

The BCG Matrix

The BCG matrix can operate at a number of levels including:

■ Corporate
■ Product
■ SBU (strategic business unit)

It is based on the principle that cash not profits drive a product from one box to another within the matrix and helps an organisation to develop its growth strategies. Its based on two dimensional variables:

■ Relative market share
■ Market growth rate

Market share is measured against the products nearest competitor, i.e. the degree of dominance the competitor enjoys, while market growth reflects the potential market opportunities and also indicates the organisations likely cash needs.

	High		Low
High	Stars	Question marks (problem children)	
	Modest + or − cashflow	Large negative cashflow	
Market growth	Cash cows	DOGS	
	Large positive cashflow	Modest + or − cashflow	
Low	High	Relative market share	Low

THE ROLE OF BRANDING AND BRANDING STRATEGIES

Chapter 3

LEARNING OUTCOMES

➡ Evaluate the role and importance of branding
➡ Analyse and apply various branding strategies in different organisational contexts
➡ Assess the issues and challenges faced by organisations in building and maintaining a global brand

KEY REVISION POINTS

➡ Branding and branding categories
➡ The role of global brands
➡ Adaption or standardisation of brands

Syllabus reference: 1.2 and 1.3

Branding – A Definition

Kotler (1999) suggests that a brand is a name, term, sign, symbol or design, or a combination of these that identifies the goods or services of one seller or group of sellers and differentiates them from the competition.

Blythe (2006) defines 'branding as the culmination of a range of activities across the whole, leading to a brand that conveys a whole set of messages to the consumer about quality, price, expected performance and status.

Branding Categories

Organisations can categorise their brands into three:

- Manufacturer (corporate brand)
- Own-label
- Generic

Brand Values

Brand values are 'the emotional benefits and less tangible identifiers attached to the brand providing reassurance and creditability for targeted consumers, supplementing the specific brand attributes in making the brand attractive'. Brand values support the more visible attributes that organisations demonstrate in their brands and can be important when the consumer is thinking of making a purchase, i.e. are the organisations values understood and in keeping with the purchasers own values?

Global Brands

Standardisation of products generally produces economies of scale which, given the high costs involved in product development, encourages expansion beyond the home market into, initially, a

Successful brands

De Pelsmacker et. al., 2004

few and then an ever-increasing number of overseas markets. However, organisations take different approaches to brandings; some believe that the benefits of a single global brand outweigh the benefits of country-specific brands with their own brand identities.

Adaptation or Standardisation of Brands

Adaptation versus standardisation

Different customer needs	Large number of buyer similarities
Infrastructure variation	Easier to control campaigns from a central source
Varying levels of education	Technology advances allow consistent brand image to be maintained
Economic, cultural and political conditions vary	Economies of scale
Inconsistent local management experience, abilities and skills	

PRICING, PRICING CONCEPTS AND PRICE SETTING

Chapter 4

LEARNING OUTCOMES

➟ Analyse the role of pricing in influencing customers
➟ Evaluate and apply a range of pricing approaches and strategies
➟ Examine the factors that influence goods and services in both domestic and international markets

KEY REVISION POINTS

➟ Pricing decisions and product pricing strategies
➟ Identification of pricing frameworks
➟ Pricing for international markets

Syllabus reference: 1.4, 1.5 and 1.6

Pricing Decisions

The six key factors to consider when making pricing decisions are:

1. Pricing objectives	What are the pricing objectives which will support the business objectives?
2. Buyers' perception	What does the price mean to the customer?
3. Perceived value for money	What benefit will the customer receive as a result of buying the product?
4. The competition	How are our competitors pricing their products?
5. Marketing mix	Does our pricing reflect the other elements of the marketing mix? Does the marketing mix reflect the price?
6. Channel members	What are the implications of price for the members of the distribution channel?

Pricing Strategies

Organisations can adopt the following two generic pricing strategies.

Skimming

This is where a high initial price is set to 'skim' income from those buyers who are prepared to purchase at this price. Buyers will be from small and profitable market segments. Apple launched its iPhone in this way, a high price was set and product availability was through a specific telephone network (rather than being available on all networks).

Penetration

Instead of charging a high price, the price is set below the price of any competing brands which may be in the market or about to enter the market. The intention here is to attract a large number of buyers in order to achieve a substantial share of the market quickly, or take share aware from competitors, or a combination of both.

Product Pricing Strategies

Market skimming	Market penetration
■ High price charged ■ 'Just' worthwhile for some segments to adopt product ■ Increased competition keeps price low	■ Low initial price charged ■ Attracts large sales volumes quickly ■ High sales volumes reduce costs ■ Economies of scale achieved

Pricing Frameworks

The broad pricing frameworks are:

Pricing framework	Summary
1. Cost based	There are two approaches: cost plus and mark-up pricing.
2. Customer based	This includes: psychological pricing, promotional pricing, differential, product-line and promotional pricing.
3. Competitor based	Pricing near or away from the competition.
4. Professional pricing	The price does not relate to the time taken to provide the service.

Price Elasticity of Demand

Price elasticity of demand is a measure of consumer sensitivity to changes made to the price of a product and organisations need to understand the relationship in order to manage demand.

There are three forms of elasticity of demand:

- Products are said to have elastic demand where a small increase in price produces a large percentage decrease in demand.
- Inelastic demand is where a small percentage increase in price produces a very small percentage change in demand.
- Unitary demand is where the percentage change in price results in an identical change in the demanded.

International Markets

Pricing for international markets offers the same options as the domestic market, but there are other factors which need to be taken into consideration.

The international distribution channel is going to be more complex than an entirely domestic one and this must be recognised when considering pricing.

Factors which need to be taken into consideration when setting different prices for each market include the following:

External

- Economic conditions, which may allow a greater (or less) price to be charged
- Level and strength/of competition in each market
- Currency exchange rates operating between markets
- Legal implications, i.e. selling below cost price on the overseas market

Internal

■ Marketing objectives for each market
■ Customer perceptions of your brand
■ Products position within the PLC

Doole and Lowe (2008) suggest the following additional factors which need to be considered as part of the international pricing decision:

■ Economies of scale should reduce the product costs

■ Markets can be cross-subsidised
■ Different segments require the marketing mix to be adjusted
■ Global trading requires a continuous need to source products at the lowest cost from around the world

CHANNEL MANAGEMENT, DISTRIBUTION STRATEGIES AND CONTROL

Chapter 5

LEARNING OUTCOMES

➡ Evaluate different channel management and distribution strategies
➡ Apply management controls to different types of channels domestically and internationally

Syllabus reference: 2.1 and 2.2

KEY REVISION POINTS

➡ Key functions of a distribution channel
➡ Different types of channel structure
➡ Distribution strategies
➡ Marketing mix considerations in a distribution channel
➡ The benchmarking process
➡ New and emerging channels

Distribution Channels

Distribution channels refer to a group of individuals or organisations (intermediaries) that move goods from the producer to the consumer or industrial user of the product. In other words, a distribution channel is the way an organisation gets its product to the consumer. Sometimes, distribution channels are referred as marketing channels. The distribution of products to consumers has two main management components:

■ Getting the tangible or physical products to the customers (the supply chain)
■ Controlling the flow of communication between the various parties that make up the distribution channel

Functions of a Distribution Channel

Functions of distribution channels	Summary
Creating utility	This refers to time, place, possession and form.
	■ Getting the product to the customer at a time when they actually want it.
	■ Making the product available where the customer wants to buy it.
	■ Giving the customer the legal right to use the product.
	■ Assembling the product to the format wanted by the customer.

Facilitating exchange efficiencies	Using intermediaries can reduce the distribution costs by eliminating, for example, many of the journeys that would take place. A manufacturer of washing machines would save costs by using an intermediary (also distributing products for other manufacturers) to get the product into the various retailers.
Alleviating discrepancies	Discrepancies break down into two: quantity and assortment. ■ Organisations need to produce in bulk to generate cost efficiencies. Many operate production runs turning out hundreds of thousands of the product each and every day. Retailers (depending on size) will want smaller quantities and consumers may only want 'one'. ■ In other words, the manufacturer produces far more products the typical customer can use. This is 'discrepancy in quantity'. A discrepancy in assortment relates to the fact that a consumer generally wants a number of products which constitute an assortment. However, a manufacture may only produce a small range of products (assortment) which produces the discrepancy.
Standardising transactions	Products, packaging, pricing and delivery is standardised through the channel.
Customer service	The intermediary will be providing service to other members of the channel or the end-user. Wholesalers will be expected to advise the retailer on any technical issue. Retailers or distributors will be expected to deal with customer enquires and deal with any issues which may arise.

Distribution Strategy

A key consideration in establishing the 'right' channels is the concept of market coverage. Brassington and Pettitt (2006) suggest that market coverage is 'about reaching the end customer as cost effectively and efficiently as possible, while maximising customer satisfaction'. Having decided on the types of distributor, the manufacture now has to select the type of distribution to be undertaken.

To achieve market coverage, there are three strategies which need to be considered:

■ Selective, where carefully chosen distributors are chosen

■ Intensive, where as many as possible distributors are chosen

■ Exclusive, where distribution is highly restricted.

Channel	Characteristics
Selective	A small number of carefully chosen distributors are selected usually within a defined geographic area. Typically this involves consumer goods, but can include industrial goods.
	An organisation will use this channel where only a small number of outlets can be handled by the organisation effectively, or the nature of the product only requires customer access in specific areas.
Intensive	Blanket coverage as the manufacturer wants as many outlets as possible to take the product, i.e. mass distribution. Generally used for convenience goods, with the rationale being to make the goods available at a place which is convenient for the customer.
Exclusive	Typically, an outlet will cover a large geographical area. Consumers tend to purchase on an infrequent basis and the product price is often expensive. Often, distributors can be franchisees.

Channel Structure

There are often relationships that exist between the channel members. The channel member can also be a member of another channel which may be a competitor to the organisation.

Relationships and potential conflicts can easily occur with the channel and, therefore, is necessary to define the structure of the channel, so that all members are clear on their roles and responsibilities and are willing to cooperate with each other and will maximise the benefits of being a member of the channel.

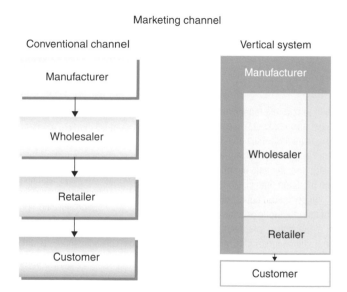

Marketing channel

Conventional channel

- Manufacturer
- Wholesaler
- Retailer
- Customer

Vertical system

- Manufacturer
- Wholesaler
- Retailer
- Customer

Marketing Tools

To be effective, an organisation must design the marketing mix to offer synergy and consistency with its channel members.

Where the organisation has overseas markets, there is the additional dimension of whether to standardise (i.e. use the same strategy across all the markets it operates in) or adapt the strategy (i.e. have a different marketing strategy for each country).

The effective use of the marketing mix will:

- Build profitable and different relationships with intermediaries
- Establish one-to-one communications and dialogue

Marketing mix considerations include:

Product	Can be a physical product, idea or service.
Price	Usually negotiated for channel member, but may be set for end-user.
Place	Range of channels depending on B2B or B2C. Internet can be used to cross both channels. Length of channel will depend on the nature of the product.
Promotion	Branding and heavy adverting is necessary in the FMCG (Fast Moving Consumer Goods) sector, along with push and pull strategies. More complex products would require trade advertising and extranet support.
People	High degree of training with carefully selected and accountable staff.
Process	Clear processes which are well-documented and have clear timescales for completion.
Physical evidence	Internal and external appearances of any buildings need to reflect the product qualities, similarly through brochures and the web.

Managing Channel Relationships

In selecting a new channel or evaluating an existing channel, the organisation will have carefully considered the cost incurred in setting up the channel, the ability of the channel to effectively distribute the products, the characteristics of the product and, of course, the customer.

While organisations understand the importance of managing costs, it is only one of a range of measures which can be used to monitor the performance of channels.

Cateora (1993) offers a framework for evaluation based on 5C's which are applicable to both the domestic and international markets.

- *Coverage*: How well the channel performs in achieving sales, market share or penetration of the market.
- *Character*: Compatibility of the channel with the organisations desired positioning for the product.
- *Continuity*: How loyal the various channel members are and the length of time they have been a part of the channel.
- *Control*: How well the organisation is able to control the marketing programmes within the channel; this can be of particular concern where long international channels are involved.
- *Cost*: This will cover the cost of investment, variable costs and expenditure.

Benchmarking

Is the process of comparing the cost, time or quality of company products against that of another organisation which is usually best in class or a competitor. Knowing how you compare is a useful way for an organisation to identify ways to improve product quality or performance in order to gain more business.

There are various types of benchmarking including:

- *Process benchmarking*: Looking at a competitors processes and identifying the best practice. It is also necessary to apply some estimated costings to the processes being observed.
- *Financial benchmarking*: Undertaking a financial in order to establish overall competitiveness; assess your overall competitiveness.
- *Performance benchmarking*: Establishing the competitive position by evaluating competitor products with similar and different distribution channels.
- *Product benchmarking*: Identifying competitor products to secure ideas for new products of your own.
- *Functional benchmarking*: Focusing on the channel or a single aspect of it such as finance or logistics.

New and Emerging Channels

The cost of setting up a new distribution channel is costly and time consuming. A manufacturer who opens a new channel to market risks upsetting an existing channel member if the processes is not handled sensitively and in line with any agreements in place.

The concept of emerging channels is fundamentally different and can radically change the way in which products are distributed and sold.

The 'corner shop' once operated by individuals who served the needs of the local economy is being replaced by the main UK supermarkets.

E-marketing has brought about disintermediation, i.e. eliminating channel members who no longer have a role to play. The Internet has brought a new type of intermediary who 'aggregates' products in one place and this in turn has brought about re-intermediation, i.e. the addition of a new channel member.

INTERMEDIARIES

Chapter 6

LEARNING OUTCOMES

➡ Examine the various types of intermediaries in the distribution channel
➡ Assess the role and responsibilities of intermediaries

KEY REVISION POINTS

➡ Types of intermediaries
➡ The role of intermediaries
➡ How intermediaries impact on profit margins?

Syllabus reference: 2.3 and 2.4

Type of Intermediaries

An intermediary is an organisation or individual through which goods pass on their way from the manufacturing organisation to the consumer.

There are different types of intermediary and each intermediary has a different role to fulfil which may also include taking legal ownership of the goods, adding some form of value which could be customer service, volume, i.e. storing goods and/or then selling smaller quantities to other intermediaries or the end-user.

Wholesalers	Wholesalers can be categorised into: ■ Merchant wholesalers ■ Full-service wholesalers ■ Wholesale merchants ■ Industrial distributors ■ Limited-service wholesalers ■ Cash and carry ■ Mail order
Retailers	Takes ownership and physical possession and sells directly to the consumer. Retailers vary in size, product and location. Examples of retailers include: supermarkets, department stores and convenience stores.

Distributors/dealers	Distributors sell products in a defined geographical area and can add value to the product by making it available locally to the consumer.
	Dealers add value by offering their expertise as well as representing the manufacturer.
Franchisees	The most common franchise allows the franchisee to sell a specific product or service in return for a payment (fixed fee, percentage of turnover or both).
Licensee	Typically, the licensee is given the right to operate a business for an organisation within a given area.
Agents/brokers	They act on behalf of the organisation, but will not take ownership or legal title to the product. They generate wider distribution and make the product more accessible to the customer. Term includes:

- Brokers
- Agents
- Manufacturer's agent
- Selling agent
- Purchasing agent
- Commission merchants

The Role of Intermediaries

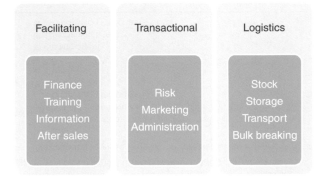

Facilitating	Transactional	Logistics
Finance	Risk	Stock
Training	Marketing	Storage
Information	Administration	Transport
After sales		Bulk breaking

Impact of Intermediaries on Profitability

Intermediaries can impact on profitability in the following ways:

- *Increased sales*: the intermediary will have its own sales team with an expert knowledge of the domestic and overseas markets.
- As the intermediary will often take ownership of the goods, it will also take responsibility for taking stock away from the manufacturer, so if goods do not sell, this will not impact on the manufacturers profits.
- Packaging together of groups of products to widen customer choice and appeal.
- Efficiency, rather than dealing with possibly hundreds of retailer, distribution and hence control can be managed through a few, for example, wholesalers.
- Warehousing and transport costs can be shared with other organisations, which may also eliminate the need for purpose built facilities.
- The value added by the intermediary may allow the price of the product to be premium priced.

STAKEHOLDERS

Chapter
7

LEARNING OUTCOMES

➡ Analyse the role of stakeholders within the distribution channel
➡ Examine the factors which cause conflict in both domestic and international channels

Syllabus reference: 2.5

KEY REVISION POINTS

➡ Stakeholders and their needs
➡ The six markets framework
➡ Stakeholder power
➡ Managing conflict in the channel
➡ Communication within the channel

What are Stakeholders?

Stakeholders are 'individuals or groups who depend on the organisation to fulfil their own goals and on whom, in turn, the organisation itself depends upon'.

Stakeholders can be categorised into three major groups:

- Internal
- Connected
- External

Stakeholder Needs

The table below sets out the generic needs of stakeholders.

Suppliers

- Will want to build long-term relationships, so that any costs invested in the channel will be recovered with an acceptable financial margin
- Participative relationship which allows for innovation and efficiency in the systems and processes used
- Clarity of information through well-documented processes and service level agreements (SLAs) so that errors are minimised
- Clear process for tending or applying for new business
- Terms of payment clearly stated and payments made within the agreed time
- Clear CSR policy

Intermediaries

- Clear CSR policy, particularly relating to sourcing of materials
- Continuity of supply, e.g. components and parts
- Transparent remuneration policy, especially with other members of the channel
- Clear rules on competition
- Clarity on roles and responsibilities within the channel

Managing Stakeholders

The six markets framework (see below) highlights the
key stakeholder markets (sometimes referred to as
'market domains') enabling an organisation to manage
relationships more effectively. The model reflects the
fact that not all stakeholders are equally important and
a distinction must be made.

Stakeholder Power

Channels take different forms and stakeholders need to agree roles and responsibilities. Stakeholders get their power from a range of sources:

Legitimate power	This arises from any legal agreement which may have been written to formalise the relationship between the parties.
	An intermediary may have been appointed to undertake specific roles and therefore it can challenge anyone or any organisation that does not comply with the roles given to it.
	Legitimate also arises through a process of delegation where an organisation (or individual) allows their own power to be given to another party.
Expert power	The intermediary may be appointed because of the skills or knowledge they possess. An internal shipping company may be used to post products to customers, or because of the value added by the organisation.
Resource power	This refers to the management of resources by the organisation. The intermediary may have been appointed because of the availability of talent resources (people) in bringing the product more effectively to the customer.
Referent power	Here, power arises from the quality of the organisation because of its reputation in the market or the strength of its brand.
Coercive power	A dominant supplier in the distribution channel may withhold supply or work.

Conflict Management

Brassington and Pettitt (2006) suggest two different types of conflict:

Type of conflict	Summary
Manifest	Open conflict between the channel members which may potentially prevent achievement of the channel objectives/goals.
Underlying	While not overt, underlying conflict can easily develop into manifest conflict. It is important to identify the conflict at an early opportunity and take action in order to prevent the cessation of cooperation between channel members.

The following table is based on Brassington and Pettitt (2006):

Areas of conflict	Summary
Incompatible goals	Members of the channel disagree on issues, including strategy, new ways of doing things or financial returns.
Role conflict	Members of the channel cannot agree on the role each should take.
Domain differences	This concerns who should make the marketing decisions.
Perceptions of reality	Different channel members may interpret issues in different ways.
Expectations	Changed circumstances may bring about a change in the way channel members may want to do things differently in the future.

Communication in the Channel

The responsibility for communication must rest with the channel leader or a nominated party. The role of communication is to improve the overall performance of the channel network.

Communication consists of two components:

■ *Data flows*: the operational day-to-day information that flows across the channel

■ *Marketing communications*: the use of the promotional mix designed to influence the channel to take a particular course of action. Other purposes include motivation, goodwill and understanding

CONTRACTUAL REQUIREMENTS AND SERVICE LEVEL AGREEMENTS

Chapter 8

Syllabus reference: 2.6

Contractual Requirements

Restricted Sales Area

A producer will often grant a specific geographical area (postcode area, town or region) to an intermediary such as an agent or a distributor.

Tying Contract

In return for the rights to sell a particular product, producers may insist that intermediaries must purchase other items as well. Often this is done to encourage sales of weaker items; however, in some situations, a manufacturer will insist on a range of products being supplied.

Exclusive Deal

A producer may insist that an intermediary does not stock competitor products, i.e. offers an exclusive deal only .This affords the producer significant protection, but it will generally be permissible if similar products are available.

Refusal to Deal

Producers as we have seen earlier go to considerable trouble to select the right distributor for their products. Equally, they may choose not to allow certain intermediaries to distribute their products for a variety of reasons such as image or cost.

Service Level Agreement

An SLA sets out the minimum level of service a third party can expect to receive, measured against set dimensions.

The SLA has three main objectives, which are to:

- Act as a point of differentiation
- Improve quality
- Improve customer service

SLA – Costs and Benefits

■ An SLA has more appeal to the end-user if there are some financial benefits attached in the event the agreement is breached.

■ The cost and the level at which failure is deemed to occur can have a significant financial impact on the organisation delivering the service.

Measuring the Effectiveness of Intermediaries

Typical criteria for measuring the effectiveness of intermediaries include:

■ *Sales*: target levels of sales to be achieved in a given period

■ *Stock levels*: minimum levels of stock which must be maintained

■ *Delivery times*: maximum time between order and delivery

■ *Returns policy*: maximum period in which faulty goods can be returned

■ *Training programmes*: minimum number of staff to be trained on in a set period

■ *Customer service*: maximum time a telephone call can go answered, complaint handling times

■ Customer retention rates

MARKETING COMMUNICATIONS STRATEGY

Chapter 9

LEARNING OUTCOMES

➡ Examine the role of marketing communications and its strategic aims
➡ Assess the contribution of marketing communications in building relationships with stakeholders
➡ Evaluate the role of communication in securing competitive advantage
➡ Examine the legal aspects of marketing communications

KEY REVISION POINTS

➡ The components of a communications plan
➡ Global/international aspects of communication
➡ Standardisation or adaption of marketing communications
➡ Push, pull and profile strategies

Syllabus reference: 3.4 and 3.5

Alignment with Corporate Objectives

The communication objectives cannot be developed in isolation of the wider business and planning process conducted by organisations.

The marketing communications plan is set against the background of other planning tools and forms a hierarchy of interconnected activities which collectively link the process together.

The communications objectives are directly derived from the marketing objectives which in turn come from the corporate objectives, themselves coming from the mission and vision statements.

A typical hierarchy could look like this:

Corporate mission	
Corporate objectives	↓
Marketing objectives	
Marketing strategy	
Marketing communication objectives	

Marketing Communications and Marketing Communication Plans

To ensure that all parts of the organisation are focused on effective communications, a clear marketing communications plan is necessary.

Generally, organisations communicate with more than one audience and each audience may need different messages. The marketing communication plan will identify each audience and develop a different communications channel to develop a meaningful dialogue with. The plan will measure the effectiveness of individual campaigns as well as overall effectiveness.

A typical marketing communications planning framework is summarised below. However, the plan can be broken down into discreet sections:

- Context
- Objectives
- Strategy
- Integrated plans

Marketing communication plan		
1.	Context	The research programme
2.		Assumption – qualitative/quantitative
3.		Corporate objectives
4.		Marketing objectives
5.		Budget considerations
6.	Communication objectives	Marketing communication objectives
7.	Strategy	Target market
8.		Target market justification
9.		Agency selection
10.		Creative planning and execution
11.		Above/through and below the line objectives and strategy
12.	Integrated plan	Controlling the marketing communications plan
13.		Contingency planning
14.		Budget breakdown

B2B Communications

Personal selling	Allows complex products to be explained.
Trade advertising	Most industries and markets have a specific journal or newspapers.
Direct marketing	Direct mail in the B2B sector needs to be highly targeted.
Sales promotion	Tactical way to generate increased sales by offering additional incentives on selected product lines for a short period of time.
Exhibitions	Often, the focus on an organisation's new product range where potential buyers come specifically to see the season's new product range(s).
PR	Needs to be managed effectively so that the organisation is always at front of mind with customers.
Internet	Increasingly important medium. The web acts as showcase for the organisation.

Global/International Aspects of Communication

Increased internal travel coupled with the dramatic growth in the web could increasingly lead to the belief that all markets can be similarly treated and communicated with.

Type of organisation	Approach adopted
International	Countries beyond the home market receive the same marketing mix(s) as the home country.
Multinational	Individually designed marketing mix(s) for each country.
Global	One single marketing mix.

Standardisation or Adaption of Marketing Communications

Adaption
- A central theme can be tailored to the needs of the local market making it more tailored and relevant. It shows greater understanding of the individual market as the message can be developed by 'local people for local people'.
- Adapting the communication recognises that local needs do vary and a generic message may not always be appropriate. Needs wants, purchasing habits behaviours and so on vary across markets.
- Educational levels vary and 'sophisticated' messages may not always be appropriate; similarly as we have seen with the concept of culture, messages can be interpreted differently.
- Legal issues and constraints will vary across national boundaries and sometimes within countries, so what may be acceptable in one market may not be acceptable in another and similarly different codes of practice with legally or voluntarily controlled may be in place.

Standardisation

- As highlighted earlier, satellite television has broken down many barriers including culture which separated markets. Consequently, many earlier arguments for adaption are being eroded. For example, Disney has appeal in most countries and the message can be standardised.
- Locally developed campaigns have historically been perceived as being of poor quality which standardisation addressed.
- Standardisation allows for a consistent and strong brand to be developed across all markets.
- Organisations may prefer to control campaigns in each and every market centrally because they want to maintain control.
- Costs are reduced as a result of standardisation; few advertising agencies and greater production volumes all contribute to efficiency.
- Consistency, the message can be tightly controlled leading to greater brand consistency across the various markets.

Marketing Communication Strategies

There are three communication strategies which can be used across all sectors.

Push	Pushing the product into the distribution channels, e.g. through personal selling, exhibitions, sales promotion and trade advertising.
Pull	Pulling the product through by encouraging customer demand through advertising, sales promotion and in-store merchandising.
Profile	Responding to and receiving information from stakeholders.

MARKETING COMMUNICATIONS IN DIFFERENT ORGANISATIONAL CONTEXTS

Chapter 10

Internal Marketing

Internal marketing refers to the promotion of a marketing orientation throughout an organisation. Internal marketing also includes:

- Creation of customer awareness
- Quality management programmes
- Change programmes

The Internal Marketing Mix

Product	Usually relates to the changing nature of a job role.
Price	The balance of psychological costs and the benefits of adopting a new orientation.
Place	Where the activity takes place.
Promotion	External promotional methods can be adopted internally to reflect to staff the image portrayed in the market.
People	This relates to those involved in producing and delivering communication, training media and meetings.
Processes	The communication and media process by which the product is brought to the customers' attention.
Physical evidence	Training, briefings, documentation and place.

Internal Communications

Marketing communications is concerned with the way various stakeholders interact with each other and internal communications relates to the way stakeholders within an organisation communicate with each other and receive marketing attention.

Internal stakeholders are employees and management who are interested in different issues; however, it is generally accepted that employees should be the key focus of internal communication.

Roles for internal communications

DRIP	*Differentiate*: To differentiate the type and nature of communication across different employees or groups of employees. *Remind*: To remind staff of key values. *Inform*: To provide staff with information. *Persuade*: Use persuasive language or imagery to convey consistent messages.
Transactional needs	Directing new initiatives, coordinating actions or using resources efficiently and effectively.
Affiliation needs	Generating a sense of identity with the organisation as well as promoting and coordinating activities with external groups or individuals.

Internal Communication Methods

Clear and consistent messages ensure brand consistency.
  The following table offers a range of communication methods available to communicate internally.

Intranet	The intranet is a system for distributing information electronically through its internal network. Staff can access a broad range of information which can be tailored to specific groups. For example, shop floor staff may be restricted to product information and HR. Large organisations can have a number of intranets each serving the need of a particular division. Information should be kept up to date, otherwise, reliability will be questioned by the staff. Typically, the intranet will be the first screen to be seen by the staff when they open the PC in the morning.
E-mail	An impersonal but quick way to communicate with all staff. Fast and cost effective, it can be used to update staff on new developments. However, staff typically get many e-mails everyday and can be 'missed'. Staff can clarify aspects of the message if it is not understood.
Seminars	Seminars bring together small groups of people generally for recurring meetings.
Briefings	A briefing can be presented in writing or orally. Typically, a briefing is given when procedure change or significant organisational change is planned.
Newsletters	Historically, newsletters were distributed in paper format. Increasingly, newsletters are now circulated electronically.
Mobile	Increasingly, mobile phones are being used as a communication for non-voice communication. Mobile phones now have access to the Internet and staff can read e-mails, access the intranet and generally communicate internally through electronic means.

PROMOTIONAL ACTIVITY

Chapter 11

LEARNING OUTCOMES

➡ Evaluate a range of communication mixes
➡ Apply the optimal mix for internal and external marketing activities
➡ Assess creative and innovative approaches to communication activities

KEY REVISION POINTS

➡ Promotional activity
➡ Advantages/disadvantages of communication tools
➡ Setting communication objectives

Syllabus reference: 3.3

Promotional Activity

Promotional activities can also be referred to as above-, below- or through-the-line.

Above-the-Line

Above-the-line activity relates to promotional activities carried out through mass media such as press, magazines, radio, outdoor, cinemas, banners and search engines. Historically, the term is related to the payment of agency commission.

Through-the-Line

This refers to activity which involves above- and below-the-line-communications in which one form of advertising points the consumer to another form of advertising, thereby crossing the line. This can include:

- Direct marketing, direct mail catalogues, telemarketing, interactive communications, including Internet

The focus has moved from mass to more personalised communications and relationships can start to be built.

Below-the-Line

Includes sales promotion, public relations, personal selling.

The five communication tools are:

1. Advertising	Mass media is often used to create awareness or encourage trial.
2. Sales promotion	Used to encourage trial or increase usage – tactical and flexible.
3. Public relations (includes sponsorship)	PR is not paid for, but often requires agency involvement which can be expensive.
4. Personal selling	Common in retail or business-to-business marketing. Expensive, but often needed when complex products are involved.
5. Direct marketing	Increasingly popular tool which can deliver personalised messages.

Evaluation of cinema advertising

Advantages	Disadvantages
■ High audio and visual impact	■ High cost
■ Captive audience and so high degree of control; audience not able to 'skim' of 'flick over'	■ Can be low exposure, i.e. low capacity in some screens
■ Segmentation is possible by area or region	■ Measurement is hard to evaluate
■ Good medium for the 'younger' market	■ Timings depend on local cinema

Evaluation of Internet advertising

Advantages	Disadvantages
■ Relatively inexpensive to set-up ■ Speed of set-up can be fast ■ Global reach ■ Creative and interactive options are available ■ Messages can be downloaded for later consumption ■ Speed of getting message to the consumer is very fast	■ Some issues about intrusion ■ Still developing medium and not yet mainstream, but growing rapidly ■ Often easy to delete the message without viewing ■ Not regulated as yet

Evaluation of magazine advertising

Advantages	Disadvantages
■ Wide range of specialist titles allowing for effective segmentation ■ Can be read frequently, i.e. more than once ■ Readership often greater than circulation (waiting rooms, hotels, etc.) ■ Long life cycle	■ Can be long lead in times especially with specialist and trade journals ■ Can be expensive when compared with other media ■ Often involves high quality (expensive) production

Evaluation of newspaper advertising

Advantages	Disadvantages
Regional	
■ High local readership, often multiple reads	■ Generally weekly
■ Low cost production	■ Often not seen as objective
■ Focused on the local area, so will have specialist sections	

National daily papers

Advantages	Disadvantages
■ High levels of readership, so mass market	■ High number of competing adverts, so 'stand out' harder to achieve
■ Short lead in times for media is very responsive to timescales	■ Limited life span
■ Range of newspaper titles, so segmentation can be effective	■ Generally need a campaign rather than a 'one off' advert
■ Wide choice of advertising options, e.g. main newspaper (and choice of positioning and size) or specialist section	■ Production costs can be high

Evaluation of outdoor media

Advantages	Disadvantages
■ Repeat exposure, generally we go to work the same way or shop in the same area ■ Supportive of other media, i.e. reinforces messages ■ Flexible duration of campaign	■ Opportunity to see poster can be quite short if passing in car, train or bus ■ Random viewing by people

Evaluation of radio advertising

Advantages	Disadvantages
■ Cheap (cost per listener) ■ Can have large coverage ■ Can link in with sponsorship ■ Can be targeted ■ Portable, i.e. variety of listening locations, e.g. car, home, shop	■ Radio can 'background', so not actively listened to ■ Generally ads last a few seconds only, so need repeating ■ Creativity currently restricted because of the media, but DAB radio has increasing opportunities

Evaluation of TV advertising

Advantages	Disadvantages
■ High impact	■ High cost
■ Mass audiences, so wide coverage quickly	■ Can channel-hop and avoid the ads
■ High degree of creativity is available	■ High risk, if ads are poorly constructed in terms of message and tone
■ Strong sound and visual qualities	■ Can have long production times
■ Evaluation mechanisms are well developed	

	Advertising	Sales promotion	Public relations	Personal selling	Direct marketing
Absolute costs	High	Medium	Low	High	Medium
Cost per contact	Low	Medium	Low	Low	High
Wastage	High	Medium	High	High	Low
Size of investment	High	Medium	Low	High	Medium

	Advertising	Sales promotion	Public relations	Personal selling	Direct marketing
Ability to target particular audiences	Medium	High	Low	Medium	High
Management's ability to adapt quickly as circumstances change	Medium	High	Low	Medium	High

Setting Marketing Communication Objectives

Often, accountants will suggest that promotional activity is a cost to the organisation and the counter argument from the communications team is that it is an investment in the business. Both can be right if the communication team cannot demonstrate the benefit of the campaign or activity.

Setting objectives is important to an organisation for the following reasons:

■ A method of communication and coordination between different groups with the intention that performance will be improved through a common understanding

■ A guide to decision-making

■ A focus for decision-making in the campaign

■ A benchmark to measure performance against

To help organisations to set objectives, guidelines generally referred to as SMART objectives have been established.

SMART objectives require an organisation to carefully consider what the desired outcomes of the communication activity need to be. In other words what is to be achieved, when does it need to be achieved by and who is it aimed at?

The following table is adapted from Fill (2005):

Specific	What is the specific variable that the organisation wants to influence in the campaign? Is it sales, perception, attitude, awareness, etc.? The variable must be clearly defined and clear outcomes established.
Measurable	How is the activity going to be measured? For example, are additional sales achieved during a set period? The number of telephone calls received at the call centre?
Achievable	Objectives must be attainable, otherwise failure will simply demotivate staff and be a waste of effort (and money).
Realistic	Objectives should be based on research or market intelligence and be relevant to the brand.
Targeted/timed	Who is the audience for the activity and over what period are the results to be achieved?

AGENCY AND AGENCY RELATIONSHIPS

Chapter 12

Syllabus reference: 3.5–3.7

Communications Agencies

An organisation has a range of agency types to choose from. Here we focus on creative agencies, of which there are four main types.

Full-service agency
As the name may suggest, this type of agency offers the complete range of products and services which a client may need to advertise its products eg. research, strategic planning, creative, media planning and buying planning.
Where the agency does not have all the skills in-house, it will sub-contract some of the work to other agencies.

Media independents
Media independents provide specialist media services such as planning, buying and evaluation. The agency will suggest the media, the size of the advertisement, location and they provide a report on the effectiveness of the campaign.
It should be noted that media dependants will be part of a full-service agency, while media independents will be separate organisations who are free to set their own direction.

À la carte
A client may choose to select a number of agencies to carry out its communication activities. Each will bselected for its particular area of expertise, so strategic planning, media buying or creative. While this may offer the perceived advantage of specialism, it does mean that the client must take responsibility for managing and coordinating the various agencies and their activities.

New media
This area has grown over the past few years and will continue to grow as technology continues to change the way organisations communicate with stakeholders.
Online brands, mobile communications, e-mail, viral marketing are all growing areas which require a specialist approach. Equally, the integration of online and offline marketing will require a greater blend of skills.

Creative shops
The creative shop ('hotshops') is an offshoot of the full-service agency. They have been formed by staff who have left full-service agencies to create a particular style or approach.

Agency Selection

The appointment of an agency is an important and formal process which is time intensive.

Selection starts with research. The following process assumes that the organisation is undertaking the selection process on its own. However, a search on the Internet will reveal that there are organisations that will assist a client in the selection, i.e. act as a consultant.

There are industry magazines and publications which list agencies according to the services offered. 'Campaign portfolio' and the 'Advertising Agency Roster' are useful starting points as they offer full contact information.

From the list available, a number of agencies should be long listed with a view to reducing the number of agencies to a more manageable number of around 10.

Shortlist criteria

1.	Area of expertise held by the agencies
2.	Quality of existing clients (need to consider any competitive issues)
3.	Reputation of principals and experience of staff
4.	Agency fees and methods of charging
5.	In-house resources

Agency Remuneration

There are four ways in which an agency can be rewarded for its efforts on behalf of its client. The three methods are listed below, with the fourth option being a combination of methods.

Reward method	Explanation
Commission	Traditionally, agencies were paid a commission in exchange for using a particular publication. Commission was paid at a rate of 15%. However, different agencies received different levels and clients increasingly became concerned about agency objectivity when planning media schedules. Consequently, the fee payment method became more popular and the concept of payment by results gained popularity.
Fees	Whatever media is chosen, payment is by a set fee for a particular activity. Monthly fees irrespective of the work put through the agency will be paid, known as retainer. In addition to the retainer, a fixed price will be agreed for each component of a campaign. For example, a client may agree a fixed monthly fee in addition to a menu of prices for specific activity.
Payment by results	While popular overseas, it is used selectively in the United Kingdom. Depending on the success of the campaign, different payment terms will be triggered. While many would argue the merits of the approach, an agency can argue that success is hard to define and in any event, elements of the campaign maybe outside its control.

Managing Agencies

Beltramini and Pitta (1991) suggest four benefits of effective relationships with agencies:

1. Agencies must have a genuine interest in meeting the needs of the client in order to demonstrate a commitment to maintaining a productive relationship. The agency must always respond to any concerns raised by the clients and it needs to be recognised that relationships can take time to build. Therefore, care should be exercised by the client when considering changing agencies.

2. The relationship between the parties often requires sensitive information to be shared and consequently the agency views privileged information which offers an insight into the nature of the client which may not be ever seen by the customer. The agency should invest time in understanding the client, its DMU and its structure.

3. Close relationships need to be maintained between the key players in the agency and the client at both the strategic and operational levels.

4. There needs to be two-way communication between the parties and the agency needs to ensure a constant flow of ideas from the client.

The Communication Brief

Objectives	■ What objectives have been set for the campaign and how will they be measured, i.e. sales conversion of leads into prospects?
	■ What behavioural or attitudinal measures will be used and over what timescale?
	■ How does the activity support the overall brand promise?
	■ Does the campaign form part of a wider campaign and if so how does it fit in?
Target audience	■ Who is the audience?
Product	■ Description, positioning and features.
	■ Any conditions for application?
	■ Key competitors.
	■ Why should people buy this product?
	■ USPs.
Creative and media considerations	■ Research undertaken on current creative work?
Logistical considerations	■ Any media constraints?
Budget	■ Exactly what does the budget cover?

CUSTOMER SERVICE AND CUSTOMER CARE PLANS

Chapter 13

LEARNING OUTCOMES

➡ Examine the importance of customer service
➡ Assess the value, importance and financial implications of customer service
➡ Examine the costs involved in providing customer service

KEY REVISION POINTS

➡ What are services?
➡ The extended marketing mix
➡ Using the marketing mix to overcome the issues of service

Syllabus reference: 4.1–4.3

What are Services?

Services are referred to as being 'intangible' and consist of industries such as banking, insurance, government, education, professional services and tourism. Services embrace the non-profit sectors and can be intended to satisfy both business and personal customer needs.

There are many definitions of a service. Kotler et al. (1999) defines a service as 'any activity or benefit that one party can offer to another which is essentially intangible and does not result in the ownership of anything'.

The Marketing Mix for Services

The concept of the marketing mix (Borden, 1964) consists of four elements which when combined together create an offering for the customer. The mix known as the 4Ps (product, price, place, promotion) is not sufficient for the service sector and 3 additional Ps was proposed by Booms and Bitner (1981) which is now generally referred to as the 7Ps.

The additional Ps are:

- People
- Processes
- Physical evidence

Each of the additional Ps is discussed in more detail below.

People

Services typically require people to deliver them, often having just created them. Consequently for many customers 'people' represent the brand and where a relationship builds, it becomes difficult for a competitor to take the business away from that organisation.

Processes

Processes refer to the actual delivery as well as the support in the provision of the service.

Physical evidence

This relates to the tangible aspects of the services.

Using the Marketing Mix to Overcome Service Issues

Product	What is the collection of benefits that the product offers? Organisations offering services will still break the product into ranges. A chain of leisure centres may choose to market each one as a separate product.
Price	What does our price represent? Are we premium priced to reflect the high quality of the product? Do we price differently for different product? Airlines historically charged a lower price as the date of the flight got closer. Ryanair and easyjet changed that and offered cheaper prices the earlier the booking was made.
Place	Where is the product to be delivered? Physical evidence is closely related to place and should reflect on the quality of service. The consumption of services can take place in hundreds of different places from the dentist's chair to high in the sky. The Internet is also changing the place of consumption.
Promotion	The promotional activity must reflect the positioning the product occupies in the consumers' mind based on reputation, quality and reliability.
People	Staff must be trained in the organisations products and values. Where possible, staff should be empowered to ensure that customers are fully satisfied.
Processes	Processes need to be developed, so that the variability in service can be reduced.
Physical evidence	This can relate to the decoration, the staff uniforms, the style of the menus, each reflecting the brand of the organisation.

KEY ACCOUNTS

Chapter 14

➡ Apply the KAM process
➡ Examine the value of effective KAM

Syllabus reference: 4.4

➡ What are key accounts and how are they selected?
➡ KAM
➡ KAM cycle

Key Accounts

Fill (2005) defines a key account as 'customers that, in a business-to-business market are willing to enter into relationship exchanges which are of strategic importance to the focus of the organisation'.

Criteria for Selecting Accounts

It is recognised that it is much more expensive to recruit new customers than retain existing ones, so the criteria for selecting a key account has to be clear.

The table below offers some suggestions as a basis for selecting key accounts.

Key account selection criteria

Profitability: Current and historic trends.

Potential: What is the rate of growth in the future?

Annual turnover: Does it meet the threshold now, or will it at some future point?

Brand association: Does the brand convey financial or non-financial benefits?

Relationship: Will the status of being a key account lead to additional business or block out the competition?

KAM

KAM is concerned with long-term relationships and this can come about through gaining access to new markets, better ways of working or through technological development. Since KAM is fundamental to a long-term relationship, success depends on the way it is managed. Risks to the relationship will occur when the customer demands more from the relationship and of course the other way around when the supplier is not willing or able to provide the relationship originally expected.

A structure for managing the relationship needs to be put in place and Fill (2005) identified three possible organisational approaches to KAM which are summarised in the table below.

Approach	Summary
Assigning sales executives	This approach is warranted in smaller organisations and is very much 'hands on'. There is a clear point of contact, roles and responsibilities are clear and there are the added benefits of flexibility and responsiveness.
Creating a key account division	Creating a separate division can require significant structural changes, but it has the advantage of integrating the key support functions necessary in KAM.
Creating a key account sales force	Here, the decision is made to build a dedicated KAM team who can be trained to 'higher' levels in that they will offer an enhanced level of service to key accounts through a solid understanding not only of the key accounts but the markets they operate in.

KAM Cycle

Various commentators have developed models to reflect the various relationships and the following table is based on Millman and Wilson (1995).

Pre-KAM	At this stage, there is no relationship and the task is to identify accounts that meet the selection criteria and have the potential to become key accounts. An important consideration here is to establish that the various parties could work with each other.
Early KAM	The relationship has started, but it is still transactional and there is an element of testing each other out. Communication channels will be formal.
Mid-KAM	The relationship has now developed, the organisations are starting to understand each other and work proactively together.
Partnership KAM	The organisations recognise the importance of the other and first choice supplier status is achieved.
Synergistic KAM	Both organisations see themselves as one organisation where they create synergistic value in the market place.
Uncoupling KAM	At this stage and for a variety of reasons, the relationship is being terminated and procedures are put in place to 'wind down' the relationship.

SALES AND PRODUCT INFORMATION AND RISKS

Chapter 15

Syllabus reference: 4.5 and 4.6

MIS

Organisations typically collect huge amounts of information on customers, but often the information is not used because it is not in an accessible format, or it may just be old and no longer valid. This is a waste of resource and money. Organisations, irrespective of size, need to be able to collect useful information, store it and retrieve it in a timely manner so that it can not only be used to tailor offers to customers, but also measure the effectiveness of marketing activity not just against targets the organisation may have set itself as part of the planning process, but it can be used to benchmark the organisation against the market generally.

MIS Outputs

The data having been analysed and refined is now distributed, or made available to marketing managers in a predetermined format and agreed time.

Most organisations make the information available to staff electronically and the marketing decision-makers will usually specify the information needed, the format they need it in and the time required. The information is usually available as standard report, but changes can be made by re-specifying the information, or if as is the case in larger organisations by staff having access to the core data and being able to manipulate it themselves.

Each decision-maker (i.e. recipient of the information) will need to specify their data requirements.

Format/presentation of the information	Defined report in hard/soft copy
Data sources (external)	Is this Mintel reports, company/competitor websites, annual report and accounts? Industry reports, government data or economic data.
Data sources (internal)	Key account(s) purchasing trends/patterns.
Frequency of reports	Weekly/daily, etc.

Some organisations have moved beyond MIS and now use MDDS (marketing decision support systems) software which aids the decision-making process by helping managers anticipate certain outcomes based on the information available. In effect managers can interrogate the database and develop scenarios.

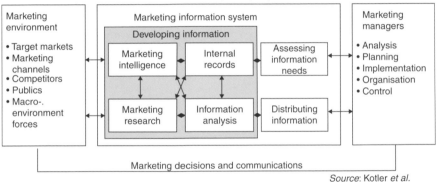

The marketing
information system (MIS)

Marketing environment
- Target markets
- Marketing channels
- Competitors
- Publics
- Macro-environment forces

Marketing information system

Developing information

Marketing intelligence

Internal records

Marketing research

Information analysis

Assessing information needs

Distributing information

Marketing managers
- Analysis
- Planning
- Implementation
- Organisation
- Control

Marketing decisions and communications

Source: Kotler *et al.*

An MIS stores and disseminates information within an organisation. In essence an MIS is a framework which allows for information to be collected from a variety of sources, both internal and external to the organisation. This information is then combined with other relevant information to produce a specific range of reports which helps the organisation manage its marketing more effectively.

Partnership Relationship Life Cycle

As products go through a life cycle, it can be argued that relationships go through a similar process. The ladder of loyalty offers one view of how a relationship develops and is managed over time. Similarly the partnership relationship life cycle offers a similar perceptive and this is summarised below.

Partnership relationship life cycle	
Partnership stage	**Initiation stage**
■ Recognition of the importance of the account to the organisation ■ Multiple relationship contacts at all levels	■ Interest generated and targets identified ■ Matching products to customer needs ■ Understanding customer needs
Consolidation stage	**Development stage**
■ Focus on building customer loyalty ■ Innovation and new product development/offering	■ Demonstration of organisations' ability to meet customer promises ■ Build resource to support the relationship